W9-BUB-282

HOW
TO BE HAPPY

52 Positive Activities
for Children

HOW
TO BE HAPPY

52 Positive Activities
for Children

Marneta Viegas

Illustrations by Nicola Wyldbore-Smith

OUR STREET
BOOKS

Winchester, UK
Washington, USA

First published by Our Street Books, 2014
Our Street Books is an imprint of John Hunt Publishing Ltd., Laurel House, Station Approach,
Alresford, Hants, SO24 9JH, UK
office1@jhpbooks.net
www.johnhuntpublishing.com
www.ourstreet-books.com

For distributor details and how to order please visit the 'Ordering' section on our website.

Text copyright: Marneta Viegas 2013

ISBN: 978 1 78279 162 1

All rights reserved. Except for brief quotations in critical articles or reviews, no part of this
book may be reproduced in any manner without prior written permission from the publishers.

The rights of Marneta Viegas as author have been asserted in accordance with the Copyright,
Designs and Patents Act 1988.

A CIP catalogue record for this book is available from the British Library.

Design: Emma Deans
Illustrations: Nicola Wyldbore-Smith

Printed and bound by CPI Group (UK) Ltd, Croydon, CR0 4YY

We operate a distinctive and ethical publishing philosophy in all
areas of our business, from our global network of authors to
production and worldwide distribution.

These are the
things I put in my
Happiness Box

My happiness box

An eraser to rub
out my mistakes

A piece of string to tie things
together when they fall apart

Rubber band
to stretch my
imagination

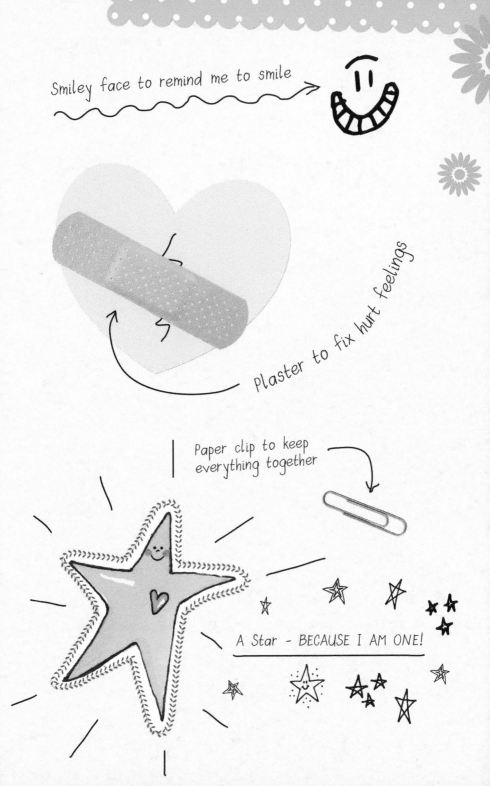

HOW TO BE HAPPY
by Marneta Viegas

52 activities for all the family

Illustrations by Nicola Wyldbore-Smith
Design by Emma Sarah Deans
Photography by nvme.co.uk

Dedication

This book is dedicated to my dear father who died 25
years ago. I used the money he left me to set up Relax
Kids instead of buying a house. I feel so delighted that
Relax Kids has brought peace and happiness to many
homes and schools and my father's legacy lives on.

Thank you, Daddy, for everything.

www.relaxkids.com

ABOUT THE AUTHOR

Marneta Viegas set up Relax Kids in 2001. She had
been running a successful children's entertainment
business for thirteen years and noticed a change
in children's behavior. Children seemed to be less
able to sit still, listen and concentrate on her show.
Using her degree in Performing Arts and techniques
she had picked up from drama, singing and mime
school combined with the meditation techniques she
had learnt as a child, Marneta created a unique
seven-step system to teach children how to relax. The
classes were a success and Marneta now runs training
for those who want to teach Relax Kids relaxation
classes to children. Marneta has trained over a
thousand people in her method from over 35 countries.
Relax Kids is now used in over half a million homes
and schools worldwide. Marneta lives in Oxfordshire
with her dog Ronnie Barker.

If you would like more information about
other Relax Kids products, relaxation
classes and to train with Marneta, visit
www.relaxkids.com

Marneta will be delighted to answer any
emails marneta@relaxkids.com

HOW TO USE THIS BOOK

This book has been created to encourage
families to enjoy quality time together
and engage in activities that cost very
little but reap huge emotional rewards,
allowing children to feel inspired,
cherished and nurtured.

These activities will help you give your
children what they crave - attention,
affection and affirmation. Activities
are designed to help nurture children's
spiritual and emotional development.

You can work through the book systematically
or choose an activity at random each week -
or whenever you have the time.

You may like to make your own scrap book
of affirmations, games and ideas.

Hello

My name is Rosie and I am 9 years old. I have a little brother called Keane and a terrier called Ronnie Barker. On some days we live with my mum and some days we live with my dad, but wherever we go, Ronnie always comes with us!

We used to all live together, but it's okay that we don't anymore because we all still get on really well and can still have a great time together as a family.

This is our little dog Ronnie. He's so cute!

This is my mum. She is beautiful and brilliant and we love spending girly time together making crafts and gossiping!

She works very high up in a big business which can be stressful, so she loves it when we get to relax together on the weekends.

This is my dad. He's really creative (like me!) and works from home as a writer. Me and my dad are like best friends and I can talk to him about anything!

Because Dad works at home, he likes to get out the house to relax, so we take lovely long walks together with my brother and Ronnie.

In this book, I have written down all the things I do to make me happy so you can try them too! There are 52 different things, which means that you can choose one thing to do each week for a whole year!
I hope you enjoy it.

I didn't write it all by myself though, my friends helped me loads by testing out the activities and making sure they are lots of fun! You can read how they got on too.

Why don't you start your own scrap book? You could write down what happened and how you felt after doing each activity in this book. You could stick in photos or draw pictures or just write nice words.
I bet you'll have loads of ideas!

Let me know how you get on!

Love, Rosie x

This is me and this is my younger brother, Keane.

P.S. -You can email me if you enjoyed the activities. Why not send your ideas and pictures to me rosie@relaxkids.com You can get lots more ideas and freebies on the Relax Kids website www.relaxkids.com

relax Kids

Contents

and some of our silly photos!

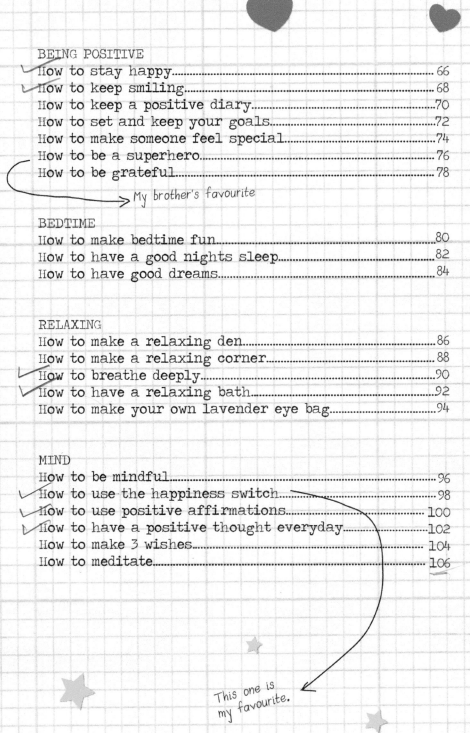

> My brother's favourite

This one is
my favourite.

How to Have a

special night.

We have a special night in our house. One with our Mum and one with our Dad. It is our special time where we get a whole evening or a couple of hours to choose exactly what we want to to do. It is such a brilliant chance to be with Mum and Dad separately and do all the things we love.

Adults call it having quality time but I just call it fun time. On the night with Mum, I get to do really fun girly things which are great and at least Dad doesn't get upset that he is not invited because I don't think he would want to do those things anyway. My Dad spends the whole evening doing boys things with my brother. I can always hear them laughing and having such fun. In summer they kick a ball about or go to the park together. I love doing special art and crafts like picture frames or cakes or watch a film with popcorn and nice treats. It is really exciting because I get to pick what we do.

I love ice-cream as a treat in summer

Sometimes I like to help Mum make some treats for everyone.

yummy!

On a Tuesday, it is time for my special night with Dad. We do things like play in the garden if it is sunny or cook a nice dinner because I am quite a good cook and Dad likes me to help him make the dinner. The best is when we make pie with mash on the top because I like using the masher and making the potato all creamy.

I really enjoy both of my special nights. Sometimes if Dad is out, my brother shares the night with me. Sometimes we both don't want to pick the same thing, so we spend an hour doing my thing and then an hour doing his. It is really good actually because then we get to have two fun things on the night than one!

They said that if they had more time, then we might have been able to have one night with Mum and Dad each, but my Dad works quite far away and they like to go to the gym and do other things, so this is how it works for us

I am special
I am special

"I really enjoyed doing this with Mummy. I felt very happy and relaxed."
Jack, Age 7.

My brother and my Dad like to play football

How to play the Secret Angels game

I love this game, it is so nice and makes me feel so wonderful because it is all about surprising people with kind and happy treats! My Mum told me that she plays it at work and that it doesn't matter how old you are, you will still enjoy it.

I told my friend about the Secret Angels game and she played it at her house. She was an angel for her younger brother, this is what she wrote about it ⟶

You could get them pretty flowers

I loved being a secret angel for my brother. It was fun to see him nd the nice things that I left for him which made him very happy. I left him nice notes around his bedroom and hid sweets in his coat pocket! Playing the game also made me feel really good, seeing him be happy because of something I did.

What you do is get everyone to-gether and put everyone's names into a hat or bowl - somewhere that you can mix them all up easily. You could ask your teacher if they want to do this with your class. It would be really good if you got somebody you weren't already friends with because it might help you make friends.

All you have to do is pick a name out of the bowl and then you are that person's secret angel and you do nice things for them for a set amount of time. It could be a month or a week, or longer! You can leave things lying around for them, like nice treats or letters or kind words or flowers, just little things that will make them smile.

A note that Mum left me in my lunch box when she was my secret angel for the day

At the end of the game, you tell everyone who you are the secret angel for. It is really fun because then you can tell each other about your nice experiences. In our house we also have a secret postbox where we leave nice notes for each other. It makes us all feel so special.

You ARE AMAZING!
I HOPE YOU HAVE A WONDERFUL DAY :)

    difference

  difference

HOW TO TALK AT THE DINNER TABLE

My family are all very chatty and we like to talk lots, but sometimes we run out of things to talk about because we see each other all the time. Do you ever get like that? Or sometimes, you just don't want to talk at all because you have spent all day talking to everyone else and you just want to be quiet. But it is important to make an effort with the people you love, even if you are tired. We decided that we should make a special effort to talk at the dinner table, because dinner time is the main time that we all get to be with each other. Then I can then have my own time later, where I can be quiet and read a book or chill out by myself.

My Mum invented this clever game that we can play at the dinner table after we've finished eating. She made lots of cards with different questions on them and put them in a jar and we pick a question and all have to answer it. It creates some brilliant conversations. Here are some of the questions:

1. What does the word SUCCESS mean to you?

2. What are the qualities that make a good friend?

3. If you could have picked your own name what would it be?

These are some of the conversation cards that my Mum made. We have them in a jar by the dinner table.

What animal would you like to b...

What is the most enjoyable thing we have done this year?

...at would ...do if you were invisible for the day?

I am interesting to talk to.
I am interesting to talk to.

If you could make a wish, what would it be?

I like being Tom. I wish all my teddies become alive! ← Tom's Wish

How to do nice things for

Mum & Dad

There are lots of nice things that we can do for our Mums and Dads to show them that we love them. Why don't you try a few of these things? They are so busy and stressed with work and being adults that they will really enjoy that you have shown them how much you care!

MOVIE NIGHT

Have a movie night - ask if you can watch their favorite film from when they were young.

You'll need one of these

Post them a card - you might have to ask for help getting a stamp, but most things that come through the post are bills and other boring letters, so this will be a lovely surprise.

SUPRISE!

Tidy the house - pick up your own toys and make the house nice for when they come in.

I LOVE YOU, Mum

My brother washing the dishes

Love letter - leave a note somewhere telling them you love them. Put it on a cereal box or on the mirror or in Mum's handbag!

Pick some flowers - don't get them from someone else's garden though!

Call the radio - ask to dedicate a song to your parents so they hear it on their way to work.

I am kind and generous.
I am kind and generous.

Favorite CD - put it in their car, so that when they turn it on it makes them smile.

How to give a Relaxing Massage

One of the nicest ways to relax is with a good massage. Some adults go to expensive salons for a massage, but I don't see why you need to pay big money or why you have to be an adult to have one - that's not fair! I think the best time of day for a massage is after a bath, because you feel nice and clean and ready for bed. I get my PJs on and then Mum gives my back a good rub and my feet a massage. Every now and again, me and my brother will massage each other because it's not really fair for Mum to always do it - even though she is best at it! She needs to relax sometimes too. When I have my feet massaged I feel like I am floating, it's so nice.

I am loving   I am loving

Here is my brother giving me a shoulder massage

The best thing about massage is that there is no wrong or right way to do it, as long as it feels nice and doesn't hurt the other person. You need to ask the other person what they like and make sure that you don't upset them. If there are more than two of you, then you can sit in a line so that you make a train. Once, we had some friends over who had not had a massage before, but they just copied me and my brother and soon got used to it and now they do it at home too!

HERE'S HOW YOU DO IT:

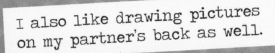

Make sure you are nice and warm in a quiet room. You can play some nice soft music.

Start very gently with a light stroke on your partner's back. Gently rub and knead. I like pretending I am kneading bread dough.

I also like drawing pictures on my partner's back as well.

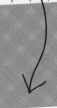

My Mum loves having her shoulders rubbed and my Dad loves the karate chopping motion. My brother loves having his feet rubbed and soft gentle circles on his palms.

HOW TO HAVE

FUN

FOR FrEE

You don't need lots of money to
have fun. Recently, my Mum and
Dad talked to me about money. I am
only young so I don't know much
about money, but it was really good
for them to talk to me because I
want to be treated like a grown
up because I am not a baby. We
normally do lots of things together
that cost money, like going out to
the bowling alley or shopping, but
they said that it can get expensive
if we do that too often. So what
they wanted us to do was think
about some things that we could to
together that didn't cost money.

My brother being silly! We were playing with things in my dressing up box!

We sat down together and came up with a list of things we could try. It was good because it has made us think about doing things that we wouldn't normally, so we have been quite creative. You might be able to think of some more ideas. If you do, let me know because I would love to try them!

There are lots of different options. Have fun trying them all!

★ Do some gardening
★ Go for a walk
★ Go for a bike ride
★ Visit somewhere important to you
★ Host a DIY concert in your garden with friends
★ Collect berries (look them up first though!)
★ Have a picnic, indoor or outdoor
★ Make pancakes
★ Look at the stars
★ Volunteer – there might be something great to do near you
★ Go to the library
★ Have a car boot sale
★ Help Mum and Dad wash the cars
★ Paint a picture
★ Make up a dance / song
★ Make sock puppets and do a performance
★ Write a story
★ Start a diary
★ Play hide and seek
★ Watch a DVD
★ Relax and have a bath
★ Listen to some calming music

I KNOW HOW TO HAVE FUN

I KNOW HOW to HAVE FUN

I love this big hat - it makes me feel all summery.

My brother can be so funny sometimes!

More dressing up photos

You could go out for a picnic - even just at the end of your garden!

How to make a Relaxing Dough

You can do what you want with the dough. I like getting the different colors and winding bits together to make snail shells and things like that! Last time, I rolled the doughs into balls and stuck them together to make a caterpillar.

You will need:
half a cup of flour
half a cup of salt
2tbsp cream of tartar
a cup of water
food coloring

Here we used cookie cutters to make shapes.

Play dough is so good for de-stressing. You get to make it into nice shapes and pictures or just give it a good squeeze to make yourself feel calmer. It's nice when you make it with your Mum or Dad or someone older, because they can do all the tricky bits that kids can't and you get to chat with them while you do it.

1 Mix the flour, salt and cream of tartar with a cup of water until you get a paste.

2 Get an adult to heat the mixture over a warm hob until it sticks together like dough.

3 Then, split the dough into a few pieces and add a few drops of the food coloring to make bright colors. We usually make yellow, red and blue, because then you can mix those colors up to make new ones.

4 To make the dough extra good for de-stressing, add a couple of drops of essential oil to make it smell nice. Lavender oil is good to help you sleep. Eucalyptus oil is good if you have a cold. Mandarin oil is good if you feel stressed.

It sounds silly but whenever we have done something like this, I feel really confident because I have made something from nothing and I have done it from scratch. I love my lavender dough the best!

I am Relaxed
I am Relaxed

HOW TO MAKE worry dolls

Sometimes I can spend a lot of my time worrying. There have been lots of changes in my life at the moment and I am finding it a bit difficult to keep myself smiling. In class, we learnt that in a place called Guatemala, children talk to their dolls and tell them their worries and then put them under their pillows at night. When they wake up, all their worries have gone and the dolls have disappeared too - like when the tooth fairy comes!

Worry dolls that my Mum bought me. I like to write my worries down or you could whisper your worries to the dolls.

We made our own worry dolls in class.
They are so easy to make!

1. Get an old wooden peg or stick. You could use a twig from the garden or one you found when walking.

2. Draw a face on it. Make it look however you want!

3. Glue a smaller stick across the peg to make its arms.

4. Wrap some wool around its arms and body, twisting it around lots of times and then tie it in a knot, so your doll has a nice woolly jumper on!

My friend has a worry tree in her room, because she doesn't really like dolls. She made it our of some branches from her garden. She writes her worries down on pieces of paper and hangs them on the tree and in the morning they are gone. It s amazing! You should try it. It will make you feel so much better!

I AM WORRY-FREE. I AM WORRY-FREE.

How to make

Worry Beads

I love making worry beads because they are so easy to make, but also because I like giving them to my friends. All you need are some nice beads and some string and away you go and make a bracelet!

We made them at home once because I was feeling really upset about something and Mum said that she had seen someone in a film fiddling with worry beads and it made them feel better.

If you use different colored beads, you can hold a bead on your bracelet and imagine passing your worry on to that bead. I put mine by my bed, so that before I go to sleep I can hold it in my hands and close my eyes and pass my worries to my worry beads.

Sometimes I sit playing with them without even realizing that I am doing it. I enjoy letting my hands fiddle with the beads as it takes my stress away. In some religions, they use beads to pray and say a prayer or special words for each bead.

My friend Olivia also likes making worry beads. Hers are very pretty.

Olivia, Age 6.

I love making my own bracelet. Now my worries are safe and sound.

I sometimes use my beads and repeat my positive affirmations for each bead - 'I am calm. I am calm. I am calm.' It really helps me feel calm and relaxed.

It definitely helps my worries. I hope it works for you!

I am carefree. I am carefree.

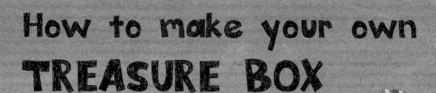

How to make your own
TREASURE BOX

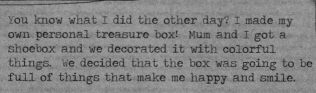

You know what I did the other day? I made my own personal treasure box! Mum and I got a shoebox and we decorated it with colorful things. We decided that the box was going to be full of things that make me happy and smile.

On the outside, we stuck pictures cut out from magazines of things that were brightly colored. I said that rainbows made me happy, so we only chose pictures of things that were the colors of the rainbow. I found some great colorful adverts and photographs. My box looked so bright and funky once we had done it.

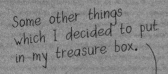

Some other things which I decided to put in my treasure box.

I put this beautiful feather in my treasure box.

Next, we filled the box with all my treasures! We put photos from the family album in and tickets from the cinema because we went to see a really funny film the other day. I found a beautiful feather on a walk the other day and put that in my box too.

We also wrote down nice words about each other and put those inside the box. It was easy to think about nice words about Mum because I love her loads and she has lots of good qualities!

This week, we are going to put something new in the box. We are going to write a story about our favorite place and think about how it makes us feel and then leave it in there. I collect lots of nice things to put in my treasure box from my Relax Kids class.

It's really nice because as time goes on I can look in it and see all the things I have collected and smile because they are all things that make me happy. The treasure box is really good for those days when I feel rubbish and grumpy!

I am unique and special
I am unique and special

How to write a *personal prayer*

My family are not religious but we do have a kind of religion that we live by and that is our family motto. Our motto is our secret little law that we have all said we will stick to. I can't tell you our motto though, because it is just for our family. Ours is a sentence that includes words that mean a lot to all of us. Do you have a family motto?

Every night before I go to bed now, I say my own little prayer and it is about being grateful for my family. At the end of the prayer I say our family motto, like I am making a promise and then I go to sleep.

Here is my prayer:

Today, I give thanks for my amazing body. I give thanks for my health. I give thanks for my food. I give thanks for my home for making me feel safe. I give thanks to my family for loving me and making me feel special. I give thanks for my friends and all the fun we have. I give thanks to nature for giving me everything I need. I give thanks for my life. I am so lucky.

Here is my brother writing
his own personal prayer.

It has become a bit of a habit now and I always do it. Even if I am going to a sleepover or something with lots of my friends, I just say it in my head to myself. The best thing about it is that it reminds me I am part of something and that makes me feel really safe wherever I am, because I feel like my family are watching over me.

I am lucky.

I am lucky.

How to make a vision board

I love making a vision board. It is a special nigh and a really nice thing to do with everybody in your family. It's a bit like making a positive picture but this time you can include your dreams and goals. My Mum's friend did once and she says it works like magic. It is all about something called positive intention. If you put all your thoughts and energy into something and put pictures up and write down what want, you can make those things can happen in your life. Someone says it's like a magnet, you just have to think about the things you want and you can attract them to you like a magnet. A vision board is great because it makes you think about what you really want in your life and keeps you motivated to stick to your goals.

To make your vision board, get a big piece of strong card and cut out pictures from magazines, old travel brochures and newspapers. Get pictures of what you would like to do as a family and where you would like to be in the future.

Here I am making my vision board.

Saving for a rainy day!

30

We had such fun making our vision board. I put a big piggy bank and some pictures of coins because I'm going to do my best to save some money. We put words of jobs that we want to be when we grow up. It really made me want to do those jobs. We even put pictures of our dream house and garden. I put pictures of nature as I love going on nature walks and my brother put pictures of sports he wants to play more. My Dad put some pictures of churches and castles. He loves history and wants to visit more places this year.

We put pictures of holidays that we want to go on and words that will make us feel good about ourselves. It's really good because it keeps us motivated and makes me look forward to the future. It also makes me enjoy now because we had fun making the board all together and working well as a team. I'm really looking forward to doing all of the things on our vision board.

I can create my future.
I can create my future.

My dream house

I would love to go sailing one day.

How to make a relaxing spray

My Mum has pretty bottles in her room and she sprays them all over herself so she smells nice. Some of them smell really strong and some of them smell like a sweet shop. I took one of her bottles, it was blue and long and had little gems on it, and I went to spray some on myself and she saw me. She said that one day I would be old enough but right now I had to learn to make my own.

We went in the garden and picked some flowers. I liked the big pink roses so we picked some of them and she picked some blue ones called violets!

I saw a really nice massive red flower in our neighbor's garden but Mum thought that the people from that house would get upset if I took that, so we just picked our own ones.

I am calm. I am calm.

Mum put 2 cups of water in a pan and boiled it and I sat at the table and took the petals off all of the flowers. When I had finished she asked me to give her the petals and she put them in the water. She boiled it all together for a while and said we had to let it cool down. then we let it cool down for a few hours. When the mixture was cold, Mum poured it through a sieve to separate the flowers and the water. She said the water that was left was my own perfume. It smelt so nice! I put a drop of pink food coloring to make it look pretty. We put the perfume in a plastic bottle that had a button on the top that made it spray out. I love it! I can't believe I have made my own perfume. I spray it on myself and close my eyes and smell it.

It was good because I could use my imagination and make new stuff

I could almost smell the flowers, they smelt really nice like a fresh breeze. When I thought about the red flower next door I really liked it because I could imagine the smell coming into our garden.

It was wonderful because I could think of a name for my perfume. I am going to call it 'Petals'. If I was going to a party or to see my friends, I would put my perfume on and ask my friends if they wanted some.

I used roses, buttercups and daffodils in my special perfume. I put it in a tiny glass bottle with a pink flower on the top.

I felt relaxed and tired when I finished.

Maddison, age 6

How to make your own fairy dust

Do you believe in fairies? I do. I think they exist all over the world, but they only come and visit you when you are a child and only if you believe in them. If you have fairy dust, you have more chance of them coming to see you because they can see fairy dust from miles away!

I believe
I believe

Fairy dust I have at home.

All you need is a little bag and some glitter or sequins or confetti. You could make a little bag out of some material or see if your Mum has one you are allowed to use. You will have to ask your Mum to get your glitter or sequins because she needs to make sure that it is safe and big enough that the fairies will see it. She will know. Mums know everything - well, almost everything! All you do is put the glitter in the bag and then when you want to make a wish, go outside and throw some in the air. Wishes come true as long as you believe in them properly.

When it was my birthday, I made some fairy dust bags for my friends to thank them for coming to my party. I gave them a card with some fairy dust in a bag inside, so that they could make their own wishes. They loved it and now they have magical dreams and make wishes all the time. It is such a good idea and will make all your friends see the power of fairies.

My friend sprinkles her fairy dust in all the dark places in her little sister's bedroom as she is scared of the monsters. Monsters can't come when there is fairy dust - it makes them sneeze!

HOW TO MAKE AN AFFIRMATION JAR

HOW TO MAKE AN AFFIRMATION JAR

This week I made an affirmation jar. I love affirmations! They are positive things you say to yourself to help you feel great. For example, 'I am happy' or 'I am special', or my favorite, 'I am brilliant!'

Even if you don't feel that way, just saying the positive words can help change your mood. I keep my affirmation jar next to my bed and whenever I need a positive thought I go to the jar and take a positive affirmation.

You could decorate your jar with stickers and ribbons.

It is so easy to make an affirmation jar! If you don't have a jar you can use a box or bag. Write out some positive affirmations on paper or card and spend some time decorating them, then put all the affirmations in the jar.

Here are some
positive affirmations
you could use:

I am amazing
I am peaceful
I am joyful
I am wonderful
I am cool
I am brilliant
I am beautiful
I am unique
I am happy
I am generous

Take an affirmation each day when you wake up
and repeat it at least three times. See if you can
remember it on the way to school. Having my positive
affirmation is like having a secret special message
in my mind and it has helped me get through some
difficult days.

It's amazing as I always seem to pick just the one that
I need! It really is like magic. At the end of the day,
I try and repeat my affirmation before I sleep.

I HAVE EVERYTHING I NEED INSIDE.
I HAVE EVERYTHING I NEED INSIDE.

When we are nice to other people, it gives us a really good feeling inside because we know that we have shared some happiness with others. We also know that when we are kind, our bodies release good chemicals that makes us feel even happier. Isn't that amazing?

There are lots of ways that I try and be kind to others, so that I can spread some love and happiness to the people that I love. It is lovely to see their faces when I have done something nice. My Mum is so happy when I help with the washing up.

HOW TO BE KIND AND THOUGHTFUL

It's also nice when you secretly do something kind for somebody but they have no idea who did it. I sometimes leave sweets in my friends' drawers and don't tell them who it's from! That always makes them so happy.

I write nice notes to my friends and parents all the time, because I want them to be surprised and make them smile. They have even started doing it back, which is really nice!

you are
Special
♡

Leave a nice message for someone

what random acts of kindness can you do?

Sometimes I go next door and help the two old ladies put their washing out and things like that because they aren't as flexible anymore and need some help. They are sisters and they are so lovely and they leave me little paintings to say thank you. My Mum does things like give her parking ticket to people if it still has money left on it and people are so surprised because they can't believe she has been so nice. They always tell her that she has made their day!

There are so many lovely things that you can do. If you are inventive, you will be able to think of more ideas. You could even leave notes on the bathroom mirror for the next person. That will make them smile. Spread some happiness, its really easy and makes you feel wonderful.

 I AM KIND AND THOUGHTFUL.
I AM KIND AND THOUGHTFUL.

How to say THANK YOU!

This is a really easy little thing to do that can make you see all the good things that have happened in your day that you might not have even noticed. Keep a positive diary and write down five good things about yourself or things that you have done well or things that have happened to you. Some days it is easier than others. If you have had a good day for example, you might be able to write down even more than five. If you have had a bad day, you might not want to write anything, but you have to try! The more you do it, the easier it will be to focus on good positive things.

thank you

Here are my 5 from yesterday:

THANK YOU

I painted a picture of my brother in Art and I thought it was good and looked like him.

My friend told me she liked my hair band.

One of the girls shouted at me and my friends in the playground, but we were cool about it because we had not done anything.

I had five fruit and vegetables today.

My Mum told me she loves me and that is nice.

THANK YOU

thank you

Mum also told me that since I have been writing in my positive diary my manners have been better because I say 'thank you' more often, so I guess it is good for her too!

Thank You

My Dad says that the more I see positive things in my life, the more positive things will happen and the less I will focus on and complain about the not-so-great things. I really do believe that!

thank you

thank you

thank you

thank you

I GIVE THANKS FOR THE GOOD THINGS IN MY LIFE.

I GIVE THANKS FOR THE GOOD THINGS IN MY LIFE.

thank you

41

♡ How to make friends ♡

The best way to make friends is to just go up to someone! I know you might feel scared about doing it, but if you just try and sit with them and ask them how they are doing then you will be able to make friends really easily. It is not hard, I promise! Especially if you can find out something that you both like.

Maybe you would like to play with them because they are playing a fun game? Then tell them! What is the worst that can happen? If they say no, then move on and talk to someone else. Sometimes there might be a new person at school who is really nervous, so you need to go up to them and make friends because they don't know anyone!

"I really enjoyed making IOU cards, but it is going to be even more fun using them with Mum!"
-Laura, age 8

Another good way to make friends is with a joke. It is a really fun way to get someone talking if you can make them laugh! If they don't laugh, then why not laugh about the fact that the joke was not as funny as you thought it would be? Have a giggle! If you are feeling brave, then you could just go up to someone and talk to them about something that you know excites them. I made friends with my best friend by talking to her about Greece because she did a show-and-tell talk about it and I was going there on holiday in the summer, so I asked her lots of questions and then I was her best friend.

Me and my friends make IOU cards. We make different ones like IOU a hug, IOU a sweet, IOU help with your homework, IOU a PJ party. They are like little promises we make to each other. We love sharing them.

Some people don't know how to make friends, so you should try and make friends with them. You never know what could happen and it could be really good and might be friends forever!

P.S. Don t forget, if you fall out with a friend, you can make friends again!

I make friends easily.

I make friends easily

HOW TO MAKE LOVE TOKENS

I made some love tokens last week. They are so easy to make and my whole family have really enjoyed using them!

To make my love tokens, I got some card and cut out some heart shapes and decorated them with different words. You could write a hug token, a cuddle token, a treat token, a time token, a giggle token and a foot rub token. You might be able to come up with some even better ones!

When you have finished, place the love tokens in a box, bag or jar. You can make up your own rules about how you use the tokens. It could be that you decide everyone gets to choose a token once a day - in the morning or when you come home from school or maybe at the dinner table. You can trade in your love token for whatever it says on the front. I had a cuddle token so I traded it with my Dad for a nice long cuddle. I love our token times as we really connect as a family.

I also made some love cheques. I got some pieces of paper and wrote promises like this: I promise to give you a 5 min massage, I promise to help tidy up, I promise to do the washing up, I promise to read your favorite book, I promise to let you watch your favorite TV program, I promise to let you have your favorite treat'. They are a lovely thing to share with everyone. I even made some for my granny and grandpa!

I LOVE *to give to others.*

I love TO GIVE TO OTHERS.

Here is my bowl of love tokens that I made.

45

HOW TO STAY CALM

Sometimes I find it really difficult to stay calm especially when everyone around me is making lots of noise. It feels like my ears are going to burst and my head feels like someone is pushing down on it really hard. Sometimes it makes me cry and when my Mum and Dad ask me what is wrong, I don't really know what to say. It's hard to explain because it's not like someone has upset me. At least when I have had a bad day at school or someone has taken one of my pens or something then I can tell my Mum and Dad why I am upset. But I don't want them to think that I am making a big fuss if nothing has happened to me.

I did find a couple of ways to keep myself calm without upsetting anybody else. Someone once told me to count to ten in my head when I need to calm down, but what I found works better for me is to think of five good things that have happened that day. I think of things that made me happy, like if someone liked my shoes that day or if I had a nice breakfast.

I also have a little book in my bag and I draw pictures inside it when I want to calm myself down. Sometimes they are not really pictures of anything, just a big scribble. Or I draw lots of little hearts and other nice things. Drawing makes me feel calmer because I have done something to take my mind off things.

I loved putting my hands on my tummy as it went up and down as it made me loads relaxed and forget other things going on in my head. Benjamin, Aged 5

calm calm calm C A L M calm calm calm CALM calm calm calm calm calm calm CALM cALM CALM calm calm calm calm calm

I also find that if I keep repeating the word CALM, I feel so much calmer inside.

If I'm at home, I can lie down with my eyes closed and try and let my head go blank for a little while. If I fall asleep then I know that I have done really well and that I must be really calm! I like lying down watching my tummy go up and down. I try and slow my breathing right down, because that's what makes me feel the calmest of all. I breathe in for the count of four and then breathe out for the count of seven. That works so well!

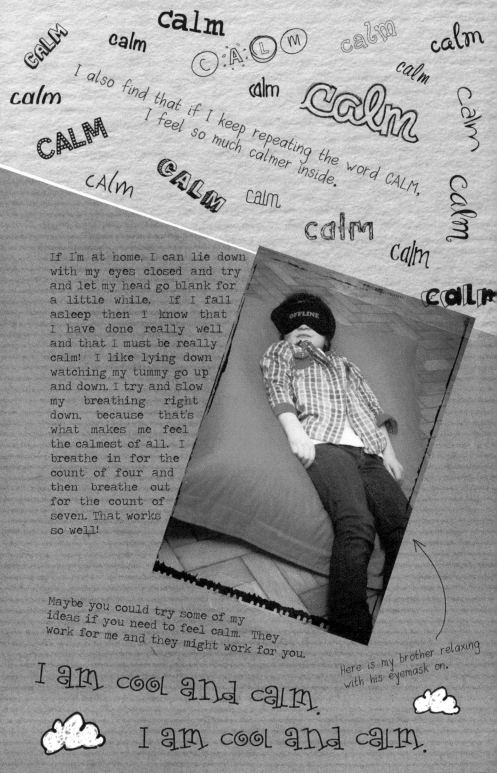

Maybe you could try some of my ideas if you need to feel calm. They work for me and they might work for you.

Here is my brother relaxing with his eyemask on.

I am cool and calm.

I am cool and calm.

How to STAY POSITIVE

This one is really, really difficult. Especially if everyone around you is in a bad mood. My Mum and Dad don't live together anymore and sometimes they argue when we are all together. I try and stay happy and be nice to everyone because I know it is hard for them too.

There are a few things that I do every day to make sure that I stay positive, even when I am feeling rubbish. First of all, when I get up, I open the curtains and look at outside. Even if it is rainy or dark I try and see something that I like about the view from my window. When it is dark, I like the shadows that are on the ground from the house next door

and when it is wet I like that I can see birds hiding from the rain. That makes me feel good straight away. When I get ready, I look in the mirror and give myself a nice compliment like, 'I like your hair today', even if I am in a mood. Then I force a smile. It is hard to be grumpy with a big grin on your cheeks. My teacher said you can actually trick your brain into being happy by smiling. I like tricking my brain.

I also like drinking from my special water bottles to stay positive. I made labels that say 'love' and 'joy' and 'peace'. Whenever I feel sad, I drink some of my 'joy' water and if I am worried I drink some 'peace' water. My Dad laughs but it really does make me feel better.

Another thing I do every day is to give myself the challenge of doing something nice for someone else. These things can be silly if you want! The other morning before school, I put a picture of a flower in the fridge for Mum, and when I got home she was so happy that it made me feel happy as well. If you share positive things with other people, it will help you stay positive too!

Everybody has good and bad days, and Mum says that no matter how bad something may seem, there is usually someone else who is not as lucky as you, so you need to be grateful for what you have and keep positive.

I am positive.
I am positive.

POSITIVITY

How to manage your moods

Moods are like the
weather and can change
all the time. But unlike the
weather, your moods are not out
of your control! Here is what I do to
manage all my different moods.

STORMY DAY - When I feel like this, I can be
angry and stroppy. My moods can be up and
down like a yo-yo. Whenever I feel myself
getting wound up on a stormy day, I notice that
I am feeling stressed and take a deep breath
and think about a time when I was in a good
mood. I think about how nice it feels to smile
and how much people like to be around me when
I am happy.

CALM DAY - When I am calm, I feel really
relaxed. I sit down and make myself
comfortable in my favourite chair in
the lounge and close my eyes and
imagine myself sitting on
this chair on the beach
and it makes me feel
even calmer.

DREARY DAY - When I feel low and grey it is
horrible. What I do is I try to imagine the sunshine
glowing in the distance and the more I focus on it,
the closer it gets and the brighter it gets until
it is so bright and warm. Sometimes the actual
sunshine really does come out. It makes me feel so
much better straight away.

BRIGHT DAY - When I feel like this, I want to share
happiness. I leave notes in peoples' drawers telling
them nice things and I skip instead of walk.

FOGGY DAY - When I feel like this, I close my eyes and listen to a relaxation
CD. I like pretending I am at the top of a mountain - far, far away!

CLOUDY DAY - When I feel like I am having a cloudy day, my head can feel heavy and muggy. So I sit down and give myself a massage on my temples. I also massage my scalp as if I am having my hair washed at the hairdressers. This makes me feel so much better and my head feels light instead of heavy.

WET DAY - When I feel like this, I go through each of my body parts and give them all a good shake. I start at the feet and work my way up to my head. Afterwards I feel more lively and ready to go!

CLEAR DAY - When I am having a clear day, I enjoy walking around and noticing all the good things around me. This is called mindfulness. It is about being in the moment and it is the best feeling ever!

CHILLY DAY - When I feel my mood is chilly, I can be a bit fidgety and always want to be busy, and so what I do is give myself a good body rub. I ask Mum to give my back a good rub and then I do my legs and feet and arms and hands and then my face. It makes me feel like I have got rid of my extra energy and calms me down.

FROSTY DAY - When I am in a frosty mood, I can be not nice to be around. What I try and do is notice that I feel that way and try and turn my bad mood into a good one. I write down my stresses to get them out of me and then think of a great thing about myself and repeat it over and over. That usually gets me out of my mood!

What do you do to change your mood?

I can manage my moods. I can manage my moods.

How to change your mood

Everyone feels moody from time to time, don't they? Sometimes, my friends or family can say the tiniest thing and it can really get me in a strop. Do you ever feel like that? I have written down some ideas that might help you if you do, so why don't you try them and see how you feel afterwards?

Go outside - When we go out with the dog, I feel great because I am getting some fresh air and some exercise too and I get to play with my dog as much as I like, which always makes me smile because I love him lots.

Go somewhere different - The other day, me and my Mum sat in a coffee shop in a bookshop all afternoon. We both picked a nice book each and we sat and read. We hardly spoke at all, but it was still really nice.

Pretend your favourite person is with you - This is really cool. You can pretend that the person you really like or a person that loves you is telling you nice things. I'm not telling who I imagine is with me!

Have a break - Sometimes things will be easy and sometimes things will be hard, but always make sure whatever is going on that you have a nice break from it all so that you can be relaxed.

Do a yoga shape - I don't know all the names of them, but sometimes when Mum is practicing with her video, I stand on one leg with my hands together like I am praying and balance for as long as I can. It makes me so calm!

Laugh - I laugh a lot anyway, but when I feel like I am going to cry, I try and make myself laugh as hard as I can. I normally end up laughing at myself, because it feels so silly!

Breathe - When you are sitting down or lying on your bed in a mood, just take a big deep breath into your tummy. It makes you slow down and stop for a bit, which is really good for you.

Use your nose - Get some lovely flowers or go and smell the ones in your garden and breathe them in. The smell will make you feel so happy.

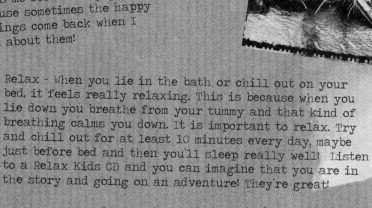

I find playing outside in the fresh air makes me feel better.

Here is my brother doing some yoga stretches.

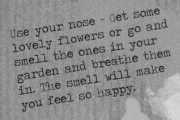

Have a chat - When I talk to my teacher or my friends, I feel better because I can get everything that is making me sad or moody out of my system. You could try this too! Talk about something that has put you in a bad mood. Then talk about a time when you felt really happy and see how you feel afterwards. That usually makes me feel really good because sometimes the happy feelings come back when I talk about them!

Relax - When you lie in the bath or chill out on your bed, it feels really relaxing. This is because when you lie down you breathe from your tummy and that kind of breathing calms you down. It is important to relax. Try and chill out for at least 10 minutes every day, maybe just before bed and then you'll sleep really well! Listen to a Relax Kids CD and you can imagine that you are in the story and going on an adventure! They're great!

I am in control of my moods. I am in control of my moods.

HOW TO MAKE MOOD STONES

When we went to the beach last year, we collected some lovely pebbles and decided that we would make some mood stones to have at home. We painted them different colors and then I decorated them with glitter pens, writing lovely positive words on them.

These are the some of words I wrote (one on each pebble):

Happy   Peace   Kindness   Play

Joy   Laugh   Magic

Fun

We have a big dish in the middle of our coffee table where we keep all the mood stones and when we feel like we need to be in a better mood, we take a stone and we think about that feeling.

We can even take that stone with us and keep that feeling all day long. They make me feel happy and confident and funny and strong, like nothing could ever hurt me.

These mood stones are like treasure and the good mood is hidden deep inside and you have to think about the mood properly for your bad mood to turn into it. What you have to do is hold the mood stone in your hand and close your eyes and think about the new mood on the stone. It's brilliant!

You could also put them all in a bag and lucky dip them and think about a different happy mood everyday. Why not keep them by your bed, so the first thing that you do is wake up and think about it? I even made some extras for my friends and they love them.

i really enjoyed decorating my mood stones. i look forward to choosing one every day! Julia, 8 years

I HAVE EVERYTHING I NEED

I HAVE EVERYTHING I NEED

These are my Mum's mood stones which she bought in a shop. She keeps them in a special little bag in her dresser.

How to not worry

I am worry free. I am worry free.

Why do people worry so much? It just makes you feel really stressed out and anxious, which is not fun! I try not to worry about little things, but sometimes I do. I just can't help it. It is only because I care! But I try to remember that worrying wastes a lot of energy that you could be doing something else with. Worrying can make you feel very bad, so you need to make sure that you take breaks from whatever is making you feel worried. Try and do some things that are fun to take your mind off it.

It's so difficult not to worry if you are worrying about someone or something that means a lot to you. My dog had an operation because he got hit by a car and I worried all day long about whether or not he would be OK. But my parents told me that it was out of my control and worrying wouldn't change anything. My dad took me for a nice dinner to take my mind off of it and when we got home, we got a call to go and pick him up. He was okay!

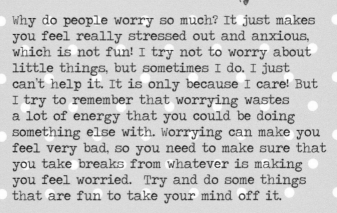

Then I felt good because I had stopped worrying and accepted that he was in hospital, and he got better!

If you start to worry about something and you can't take your mind off it, try writing it down or telling a worry doll so that you can get the worries out of you. I know that worrying won't change the situation and by getting the worries out of me, I can focus my energy on something more positive.

HOW TO CONCENTRATE

Concentrating is hard sometimes, especially when there are other things you want to do. I can feel myself not concentrating in class sometimes. I sit there tapping my pen and it's like my head goes blank and into a dream world and I think about other things and then it's the end of the class. The worst is when it is sunny outside and all I want to be doing is running around on the field and playing with my friends but instead I have to sit still in class.

It was really bad the other day, because I was in my dream world and the teacher asked me a question and I did not know the answer. She spoke to me about after it after class and she told me that when I'm not concentrating, the best thing to do is take a moment to myself, clear my head, and then I should be able to concentrate again.

My Mum always has pretty flowers in the kitchen at home. I have started practising my teacher's concentration tip in the morning at breakfast time.

I wasn't sure how to do this at first, but my teacher taught our whole class some really good concentration exercises and they have helped me so much. She told us to repeat these words over and over again:

I am focused. I can concentrate. I am still. I am quiet. I am focused. I can concentrate. I am still. I am quiet.

Then she drew a point on a Post-it note and asked the whole class and focus on that point for a few moments. If any thoughts came into our mind, we had to gently push them away and only think about the point in front of us. We had to sit still for as long as we could. It was actually quite fun!

Another exercise we did was to stare at a flower or a picture of a flower. We had to notice all the colors and textures and shapes on the flower. It was amazing how much time went past while we were concentrating.

Drink lots of fresh water to make your concentration better

She told us that it was good to drink lots of fresh water as it helps the brain function!

I CAN FOCUS WELL. I CAN FOCUS WELL.

How to cope with homework

When I am relaxed, I can do my homework much better. It stresses me out when my Mum or Dad ask me what I have got to do as soon as I get home from school. I told them this and now we have a little bit of time to relax before I start my homework and that is much better for me. I like going to my relaxation corner for a while before I start.

My Mum helps me to relax and concentrate. She makes me drink lots of water, so that I have a clear mind and puts tissues with nice oils on them in my room, so that it smells nice when I am in there. This is really good because it opens up my nose and makes me breathe properly into my tummy because I want to breathe in the nice smells.

Here I am in my relaxation corner. Sometimes I read a book or listen to music for a little while before getting on with my homework.

Sometimes if I have been sitting at my desk for ages, it really starts to hurt my lower back so I stretch to feel better. I put my feet on the ground and fall forward like a rag doll in my chair and it stretches my back.

This is also a nice stretch to do if you get an achey back.

I always try to make sure I have a nice treat waiting for me when I have finished my homework so I have something to look forward to. You should try that too!

Try to be calm about homework. It is a pain but we all have to do it, so just make it as easy as you can for yourself.

I concentrate well.

I concentrate well.

HOW TO MANAGE YOUR

Stress

The other day I got really stressed because my Dad asked me to tell him something but he was not listening. I started getting really loud and shouted lots. It really hurt my head after a while because it felt like my face was really tight and hard. I jumped about and slammed my door and the picture by the door fell down. Dad came in and said. "Calm down. I want you to relax and tell me what is wrong".

I tried to tell him but I kept getting loud and angry again, so every time I got loud he asked me to talk normally and that helped me to calm down. It was hard to keep calm because I was breathing so quickly.

He said to me that if I get stressed with something or someone because they are doing something else, I can't kick and scream about it. I have to find a way to talk properly and then people will listen.

Sometimes I like to blow on a feather to help me relax when I am feeling stressed.

Dad said he knew some activities that would help get rid of my stress. He said he gets stressed sometimes too, so we could do these things together as something for just us, which was good because I was happy to do that. We did things like stretching our hands and feeling them relax and seeing how nice it was when they were relaxed. We did things like imagining that stress was a bubble that we blew up and watched float away. That was weird because it felt like my stress was floating away with the bubble. I also imagined my stress was a big monster with a funny face. I imagined it had a funny little voice and then I imagined it was slowly shrinking while the voice got more and more squeaky. It made me giggle and I forgot my stress.

Peace... Peace... Peace... Peace... Peace...

I also like clenching my fists together as tight as I can. I squeeze my face at the same time. It feels lovely when I let go and relax.

I feel much more relaxed about stress now and when I get stressed I know what I can do about it.

I am relaxed. I am relaxed.

1. MAKE A MIND MAP - What you do is take some paper and write all the important words you can think of to do with what you are revising for. Join up the words that are linked with colorful lines so you can see that they go together. Sometime it is easier to remember images and colors, so try and picture your mind map in your test and you will have lots to write about!

This is what a mind map looks like!

You can have lots of points coming off of a main one - like this!

How to improve your memory

I have got some really good ideas to help me with my memory skills. They helped me when I was revising for some tests at school so they should help you too!

Repeat
Repeat
Repeat!

2. REPEAT - When you do things over and over, you get really good at them. This is the same with your schoolwork. The more you look at something, the better you will be able to remember it.

3. MIND BLANKS - If your mind goes blank in a test and you forget something you learned, try to relax and stay calm. Remember where you were when you were revising and what book you were writing in and what color pen you used. When you think back, you might be able to remember what you learned!

4. BODY PARTS - When you are revising, think about a part of you that you can link it with it. So then when you touch that body part in the test, it will bring it back to you!

I am brilliant.

I am brilliant.

5. LISTEN - Record your revision onto an MP3 player or write it down and have your Mum or Dad read it to you it before bed, to help it go into your head. My next-door neighbor is an actress and she listens to her lines on her MP3 player before bed and like magic, she remembers them the next day! It's amazing!

These tips really helped me, but best bit of advice that will help the most is to relax and keep calm because it is only a test and you will be OK. All that your parents and teachers want you to do is your best.

How to stay happy

Did you know - when you have happy thoughts your body sends positive feelings all around your body? It lifts you up and changes your whole attitude and makes you feel brilliant. I never knew that before, but I think that is amazing! So I guess that when we are feeling grumpy, our body would send grumpy feelings around our whole body? That sounds horrible! We must try to be happier.

Here are some ways to get you feeling good:

Be grateful - look around at all the great things that you have in your life. All of the people. All of the lovely food. All the flowers that you go past on your way to school. Just think how lucky you are to have such lovely things in your life and be thankful.

I helped my mum clean my room. It made me feel really good and happy Mandeep, Age 6

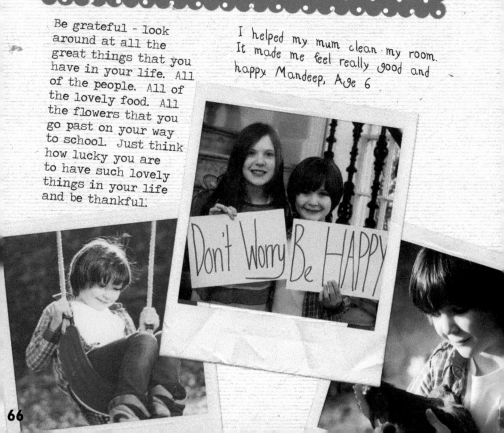

Don't Worry Be HAPPY

Friends - Think about all of the good things about your friends. Make a long list and tell them what you like about them! You will make them so happy!

Love Letters - Write yourself or someone you care about a nice letter telling them all the things that you love about them. I wrote one to myself and one to my brother. When I feel in a bad mood I read the one I wrote to myself and it makes me feel better.

Bounce - When you feel sad, just bounce on your heels, shake your shoulders and roll your head to one side and then the other. My mum does this before she goes into meetings at work and she said it always makes her feel better.

Clean your room - This is going to sound silly because cleaning is so boring, but you will make your mum happy if you do it! And also it makes you feel proud and like you have achieved something when you have finished and it looks nice!

Write your thoughts down - I have a really nice book by my bed and I write down the things that have upset me and I also write down the things that have made me smile that day, or I write dreams that I have for my future. It is so lovely, because sometimes I look back at my book and I realize I have made some of my dreams come true!

I am joyful.

I am joyful.

How to keep **smiling**

Some people walk around with grumpy faces on! You'll have seen them, walking around like the world is going to end! It can't be much fun thinking like that. Did you know that it takes more muscles to make you frown than it does to smile? Smiling is actually good for you as well.

My teacher told us that when you smile, it releases special happy feelings called endorphins. I thought that she said "dolphins" and that got everyone in class smiling and laughing! Anyway, these happy feelings are really good for your body because they help keep you healthy and act as a natural pain killer, so you don't need to have aspirins if you have a headache! It is good for your immune system, which is the part of your body that decides whether or not you will become ill. It can even help make sure that you don't get a cold! My mum went to the doctor recently and they told her if she smiled more, it would lower her blood pressure and hers is really high, so that seems like an easy way of making her better. She looks younger when she smiles and I told her that!

Another good thing about smiling is that it can really change your mood. When you are next in a grump, I want you to just smile and see if it changes your mood. It is hard to think of anything bad with a big grin on your face! I am being serious! Just do your biggest smile and you'll soon have forgotten what you were worried about!

A Poem about Happiness

Change your grumpy face into a smiley one and don't be sad
Because you have more joy when you feel good and not when you feel bad
And when you are feeling bad jump up and down
And do a funny dance like a clown
And in the morning about that time
Listen to the church bells chime
When you are sad think about who you love and care
And ask yourself what color is their hair
Next time you are feeling sad
Wash away with good feelings the word bad
So next time you are feeling sad you'll know what to do
because this poem should have given you a clue.

by Emily Jade, age 8

I am cheerful

I am cheerful.

HOW TO KEEP A POSITIVE DIARY

I know a really good activity that will keep you
smiling. It includes a bit of art and lots of
positive thinking! The activity is making a positive
diary. I got a really nice diary for my birthday
and it came with lots of stickers so that I could
make it personal to me. Mine is red and the stickers
are things like flowers and trees and rainbows and
stars and hearts. It looks really good now that I
have finished decorating it! You could buy your own
or make your own with a notebook or some loose bits
of paper.

My diary goes on my bedside table and every night
before bed, I write three good things that happened
that day inside it. Sometimes they are silly little
things but it doesn't matter, because they have made
me happy that day. I write all sorts of things
down. Yesterday, I did really well in my spelling
test and so I put that in there. The day before, my
friend bought some sweets from her holiday into
class and we were all allowed to share them, so I
wrote that down too. Sometimes, Mum and Dad ask me
what my positive things were that day and they are
good at making sure that I always remember to write
in my diary. It has been good for me because it
makes me think of good things instead of bad things
and I think that I am happier because of it too. If I
am in a bad mood, I look at my diary and it reminds
me that I am very lucky.

I find that the more I concentrate on positive things, then more positive things happen to me. It's like magic!

This is me writing in my positive diary. I like to stick in photos or make a drawing of the things that made me happy.

I AM HAPPY. I AM HAPPY.

"I loved my diary as it helped me feel good reading it even on days when some things went wrong for me." Sean age 9

How to set and keep your goals

When you set yourself a goal and then you manage to reach it, you feel so powerful and great! There are a few things that I do to help me reach my goals. First of all, I think about my goal. What is it? What do I want to do? Maybe I want to be on the school netball team or manage to eat all my vegetables at dinner. It doesn't matter what it is, but you need to decide it and then write it down. When I write my goals down it makes them seem real! After that, I think about what I need to do to reach my goal, so to help me get on the school netball team, I need to go to the club and practice my catching and shooting skills.

Here I am writing down all my goals.

The
next
thing
to do is
to write
these steps
down, and put
them somewhere
that you can see
them every day. Mine
are on my wardrobe
door, so every time I go
to the wardrobe, I see them.
Then, I think about how good
it would be to achieve my goal.
That pushes me to do my steps to
reach to my goal. Every time I do
one of my steps, I give myself a pat
on the back because I know I am a bit
closer to my goal!

I reach my goals easily.

I reach my goals easily.

How to make someone feel special

My Mum always says, 'If you don't have something nice to say, don't say anything at all'. Some children in my class say really spiteful things and it can hurt people's feelings. Saying unkind things makes people feel rubbish. I like playing a game and seeing how many nice things I can say in a day. It makes everyone else feel happy and it makes me feel happy as well.

My Dad says the more we say nice things to ourselves and others, the more it boosts our self-esteem. In our house we always try to notice all the good things about each other. The more we say positive things, the more we feel positive inside.

Here are some lovely things to say to your family and friends - can you think of any others?

I make others feel special.

I make others feel special.

This is my Mum. I like saying nice things to my Mum because she does so much for us and I think it is important to remind her how special she really is.

I like you

You are special

I love being with you

I care so much about you

You are so creative

I love you because...

You are good at...

You have a brilliant smile

You are so clever

You're beautiful

You are a real good friend

You are a star!

You are so caring

That's amazing! Well done!

Thank you for...

You make me smile

You are so important

It's fun playing with you

You are unique

I knew you could do it

You're a real super star

HOW TO BE A SUPERHERO

My dad loves watching superhero films. I would love to have superhero powers. One day, my dad told me that I can have superhero powers. Things like confidence, courage, strength, kindness, love and peace are all superhero powers. You can't see them but when you use them, they make such a difference to your life. I just have to think about a power and I feel like I have that power inside. So each day before I go to school, while I'm having breakfast I choose a superhero power to get me through the day. Sometimes it is courage or sometimes confidence, or peace or generosity.

When I'm in the car, I imagine I am wearing an invisible cape that gives me that super power. I breathe in deeply 3 times and let that super power fill every part of me. It makes me feel safe and protected. I know I can use that superpower whenever I need it.

At the end of the day, Dad always asks how I used my super power and if I needed to use it or if it helped me manage a problem.

My Relax Kids Star Cards are great for giving me ideas for my superpowers as there are so many to choose from.

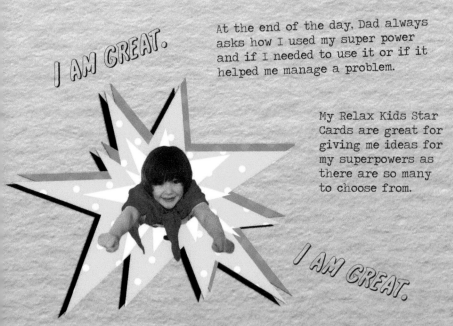

I AM GREAT.

I AM GREAT.

My brother, the superhero!!!

If I was a superhero, I would wear an orange cape of kindness to help me fly. I would wear it to school and if someone falls over I would help them get up. And I could help people by getting their shopping for them if they were too tired or sick. I'd give the kids ice-cream with chocolate topping. I feel happy when I help people.

by Tanner Campbell (TJ) aged 5.5 years

HOW TO BE GRATEFUL

Did you know that being grateful and noticing the wonderful things in our life rather than complaining about the bad can really help us feel positive?

This year we started a gratitude jar. Every day we write something we are grateful for on a piece of paper and put it in the jar. On New Year's Eve we are going to open the jar and read everything we have written. I can't wait!

This is a really good gratitude meditation that reminds me to be thankful for all the wonderful things in my life.

Our gratitude jar

Close your eyes and be very still. Take in
a deep breath and breathe all the way out.
Breathe in slowly and breathe out slowly.

Now think of all the things in your life that you are
grateful for. Think about the sunshine, the air you breathe
and the water that you drink. Think about having a home
to keep you warm and safe, and having people in your life
that love you. Think about how lucky you are to have good
food. Spend some time saying thank you quietly in your mind.

Now think about all your possessions and how lucky
you are to have clean clothes and toys. Think about
your favorite toy and feel so grateful and lucky.

Now, think about your friends that you laugh
and play with. Feel yourself smiling inside as
you think about your friends and how lucky you
are to have good friends.

Spend a few moments thinking about all the
special adventures and experiences that you
have had recently. Where have you been that
was special? What did you do that made you feel
happy? Stay still and really appreciate how
lucky you are to have these experiences.

As you sit there quietly, feel very calm
and appreciative. Feel a warm feeling of
gratitude surround you like a blanket.
Continue to breathe in and out gently as
you feel grateful and happy.

I AM GRATEFUL.

I AM GRATEFUL

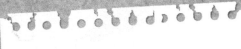

Being grateful made me feel
the actual weight of all that
I have and everyone I know.
It made me feel warm and
comfortable, until I almost
couldn't take it anymore. I
think I am getting squashed!

Jeanne, age 13

There
are lots of good ways
to make bedtime more exciting for
everyone. My little brother used to be a
bit of a pain because he used to say that he
wouldn't go to sleep, so we started doing things
to help get him to go to sleep, but I like them too!

We do things like draw pictures of what we would
like to dream about that night and sometimes we
will actually dream those things! It's weird!
My brother has a big board where Mum pins
them and we have lots of pictures up
there now.

Mum always
gives us loads of kisses
and cuddles and we do silly ones
like eskimo kisses where we rub noses,
and butterfly kisses where we flutter our
eyelashes on each others cheeks. We even do
rhino kisses, but it is funnier when we do
that with Dad, because that's when we rub
foreheads and he has a big forehead!

My Mum
always sprays lavender or
mandarin oil in the room. It smells so
nice and makes me feel really relaxed.

Mum made my brother a really nice blanket. It has
positive words all over it and he loves being tucked
under it. I think I am a bit big for it now, so that
is why he has it, but I still have nice words
on my wall above my bed.

Mum also
whispers loads of positive things
in our ears as we drift off to sleep. It feels
so lovely going to sleep listening to lovely
things. I feel really safe and loved.

Here I am, drawing what I dreamt the night before!

Here I am with a lavender eyemask.

Another really cool thing that we do is get our glow in the dark stars out and choose one and we make a wish for someone in the world. You can know who the person is or it can be someone who you have seen on the news. You can make a wish for anyone who you think needs it. In the morning, the star won't be glowing and your wish will have been granted!

I have magical dreams. I have magical dreams.

HOW TO HAVE A GOOD NIGHT'S SLEEP

Although my Mum and Dad don't live together anymore, in some ways it's really good because I have two different bedrooms! At my Mum's house I love my glow in the dark stars and at my Dad's house I have a night light that looks so pretty in the dark. I also love my pillow which has an inbuilt speaker. I take this with me so I always have it, whichever bedroom I'm in. It i perfect for listening to my Relax Kids CDs. Mum put drop of lavender oil on a tissue and tucks it insid pillowcase for me. I love smelling it as I drift of

When I get into bed, Mum or Dad reads me a story or to me about my worries for a little while. Sometime tell my worries to my worry dolls and put them und pillow. If I am feeling stressed, I hold my peace p and it makes me feel so calm.

When I'm ready to sleep, I lie on my back and put my hands on my tummy so that I can see my tummy going up and down as I breathe and it relaxes me. The other thing that my Mum makes me do sometimes if I feel too awake is to close my eyes and think of my favorite place. I am not telling you where my favorite place is, that is my secret, but it is very warm and pretty. She said if I close my eyes and think of every detail I can and concentrate on how I feel when I am there, then I will be able to sleep well.

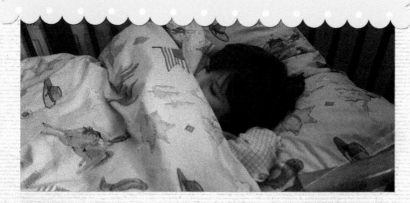

I also like repeating my affirmation very slowly in my mind. I just say, 'I am calm. I am calm. I am calm. I am calm.' Just repeating that word makes me feel calm. I feel as if I am floating on a fluffy cloud.

If you want to make sure you have a really good night's sleep, sprinkle some fairy dust around the room. The fairies will make sure you have lovely dreams!

When you sleep well, you wake up in a good mood. When you are in a good mood, everyone likes you more and you like yourself more.

I feel calm at bedtime. I feel calm at bedtime.

When I go to sleep the fairies are waiting for me in fairyland –
Ayden, age 5

It made me feel really peaceful and warm in my heart and tummy
– Jietske, age 9

How to have good dreams

I started getting nightmares a while ago and it upset me so much one night that I went in to see my Dad and asked him to help me. Dad said 'Climb back in bed and close your eyes' and stroked my head. He said stroking my head would take all of the baddies out of my head and throw them out the window.

Then he said I should put my hand in my pajama pocket and take all the goodies out and put them into my head so that I have nice dreams. He asked me what my goodies were and I told him they were ponies and princesses and he said they were perfect for having nice dreams. My brother's goodies were superheroes and wizard wands and footballs.

When I was little, Mum used to tell me to imagine that there was an invisible vacuum cleaner in the room and that it sucks away all the bad dreams and worries you have. I would go to sleep and pretend to switch on the vacuum cleaner and all my worries would go away. It was brilliant!

My friend writes down on pieces of paper what she wants to dream about. She makes a wish every night as well. I like that idea! I might try it. Maybe you could too!

Another way to make sure you have nice dreams is to read a meditation before bed. There are loads of really cool ones in my Relax Kids books where you can imagine you are a character in a story. Or you could even try making up your own. Here's one my friend wrote:

Your world is a world of white clouds. The only things that are colors are paths and roads. You see your house and your beloved family inside the cloudy house. You go inside the house and sit beside your family and snuggle in with them, you love your family.

Jude Russell

I am imaginative. I am imaginative.

How to make a relaxing den

One of my favorite things to do is to make a den. My brother likes it too! It is so much fun and I like it best when we use the things from our rooms because when my things are part of my den, it makes it even more special. My Mum lets me use my bedsheets, but she has to help me because they are so big and it is hard to do it by yourself. If you put some of the dining chairs out then you can put your bedsheet over the top of the chairs and then put pegs on it to stop it falling down. It is good if you build your den by a wall so you can rest your teddies and dollies against the wall and they will sit up when you are in the den having a tea party or telling them stories. When my friend came over we put cushions in there for us to sit on and my Mum put the lights from the Christmas tree around it so it looked like a magical tent!

I ENJOY MY OWN COMPANY.

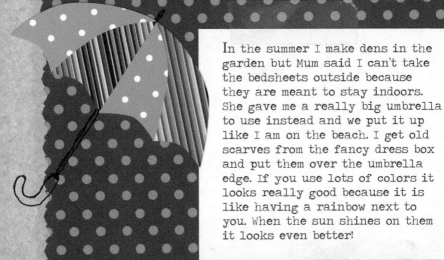

In the summer I make dens in the garden but Mum said I can't take the bedsheets outside because they are meant to stay indoors. She gave me a really big umbrella to use instead and we put it up like I am on the beach. I get old scarves from the fancy dress box and put them over the umbrella edge. If you use lots of colors it looks really good because it is like having a rainbow next to you. When the sun shines on them it looks even better!

Another thing you can do is hang blankets from the washing line and make an outdoor tent. My brother and his friends made a den with lots of cardboard boxes once. It looked so cool but I wasn't allowed in it! I don't mind spending time on my own in my den. Sometimes it's good to enjoy your own company. I love having a picnic, reading books, coloring and writing in my den.

Our indoor den me and my brother made together. We filled it with lots of soft cushions and blankets.

I ENJOY MY OWN COMPANY.

HOW TO MAKE A RELAXING CORNER

We did a really good activity the other week, we took a corner of my room and made it into my own chill out corner. This is the place I can go when I feel stressed and need to chill out.

I let members of my family share my chill out corner when they need to feel calm. Mum says she loves the chill out area as it is like going to a spa for a few moments. She likes sitting on a bean bag and listening to some calming music.

We painted the corner of the room in a soft blue because that is my favorite color and it calms me down. I have lots of cushions and a beanbag in my chill out corner and we spray nice smells around the room. We switch off the lights and use my special night light that gives a nice soft color to the room. We also have some battery-operated candles and fairy lights to make the area feel very special and peaceful. We have a small table in the chill out corner and keep very special things on the table, like affirmation cards and peace stones and other things we love. I love finding special things to add to the table, I collect lots of little bits from my Relax Kids classes!

Me and my brother in our chill out corner

I like going to the chill out area when I come home from school before I start my homework. If I am upset or angry I go there to help me calm down. My Mum sends me there for time out too. It is actually quite nice and not like punishment, but gives you time to think about what you have done and make yourself ready to say sorry.

Here is a really good relaxation to try when you need to relax. Ask someone to read it out to you as you relax in your own chill out corner.

Close your eyes, be very still and imagine you are lying down on the beach. Feel the warm sand underneath your body. You can hear the waves of the sea. Now, very gently, you are going to relax each part of your body. Start with your feet, let your toes completely relax and become soft. Let this feeling spread gently through your feet. Now squeeze your legs and gently let them go. Feel all the tension in your legs being released as they become relaxed and soft. Squeeze the muscles in your tummy and let go completely. Stretch your back as long as you can and relax. Can you feel your back sinking into the sand? Now let your shoulders and neck become soft, as all the tension melts away. Squeeze your arms as tight as you can and let them go.

Allow your arms to feel heavy as they sink into the sand. Squeeze your fingers into a tight fist, and now uncurl them slowly and rest them on the golden sand. Scrunch your face into a tiny ball and let go and relax. Let your head completely relax. Relax your eyes, your ears, your cheeks, your forehead. Become completely still and relaxed. Feel the warm sun on your face and body as you sink further into the powdery sand. Feel your whole body relaxing. You feel calm and relaxed. You feel calm and relaxed.

I AM RELAXED. I AM RELAXED.

How to breathe deeply

I heard that most adults don't know how to breathe properly.
That seems really weird to me because they are adults and
they should know how to - they have had their whole lives
to practice and get it right! My teacher said that a lot
of adults breathe from their chest because when they are
stressed, they start to panic and that's how their body
reacts. You need to breathe right down into your tummy
like a baby does when it is in bed. Babies know what they
are doing because they breathe naturally and haven't got
any bad habits! They just lie there and do it the way they
should because they don't know any different.

A really good activity that you can try
is tummy breathing. My Dad tells me to
try and keep my shoulders down when I
do it. When I breathe in, my tummy rises
and when I breathe out, it goes back down.
When I breathe into my tummy I feel calm.
I try and do it before I go into a test
or anything that makes me stressed. You
can do tummy breathing anywhere, but
you might not always be able to lie
down. When you are at the bus stop, or
at school or wherever, you might have to
imagine that there is a hula hoop around
you and every time you breathe into your
tummy, it touches the hula hoop. If you do
it when you are having an argument with
your brother, then it will calm you down
and you probably won't want to argue with
him anymore because you will be so calm.

When I am upset or feel anxious, my Mum says that deep breathing is a really good way to calm down. She said it is impossible to be stressed and upset when you breathe deeply. It's like magic - it works every time!

Sometimes to make it more fun, I try and tighten and relax different parts of my body as I breathe in and out. My best friend says she imagines her breath is a color and she breathes in that color and then breathes out that color slowly. She likes blue the best as it makes her feel very calm.

I feel lucky to be alive

I feel lucky to be alive

My Mum and I tried playing a game where we did some snake breaths. I learnt this in my Relax Kids class. You breathe in slowly and then hiss like a snake slowly and softly and whoever can keep hissing the longest has the longest snake. It is great fun!

I love noticing my breath and feeling how cool it is when I breathe in and how warm it is when I breathe out. It's really quite amazing, as breathing keeps me alive!

I loved snake breathing. It clears your mind and lets you focus on the competition to have the longest snake.

Oliver, age 10

My favourite fluffly slippers I love to wear after my bath

HOW TO HAVE A relaxing Bath

Bubble baths are so much better than ones without bubbles, don't you think? When it's bath time, I ask Mum if we have time to have a big bath. When she says yes, it's the best thing ever! She pours bubble bath under the hot water and fills it up so that I have lots of foamy, sweet bubbles in the tub. Sometimes Mum gets me some pieces of cucumber and I put them over my eyes, like I'm at a spa. It's really cold at first but if you lie there for a minute, you just get used to it and it feels nice and it cools me down.

The nicest thing is when my Mum or Dad read me a story and I just sit with my eyes shut and listen. I love imagining that I am a dolphin or mermaid floating on water.

Here are some ideas to
make your bath times
enjoyable and fun:

BUBBLES - it's such fun blowing bubbles in the bath

BATH CRAYONS - I love getting creative
with bath paints and crayons

FOOD ColorING - I sometimes
add a couple of drops of food
coloring for a colorful bath

OATS - a handful of oats added to
the water helps itchy skin

SALT - a handful of salt makes you extra sleepy

LAVENDER - two drops of lavender
in the bath is so relaxing

MILK - add a cup of milk into the bath to soften skin

TOWELS AND PJS - put your towels
and PJs on the radiator for an
extra treat when you get out

GLITTER - sprinkle body glitter into the
bath for a magical touch

After my bath
I get tired and
it's really nice
because then I
can go straight
to bed all clean
and sleepy.

I am calm. I am calm.

HOW TO MAKE YOUR OWN LAVENDER EYE BAG

Something that is really nice to do is make a lavender pillow for your eyes. When I'm feeling low, I just lie on my bed with my Relax Kids CD on and put the pillow over my eyes and relax.

WHAT YOU NEED:

- flaxseed
- lavender flowers
- some soft fabric
- scissors
- pins
- needle and thread

If you grow lavender in your garden, it will attract pretty butterflies and bees.

I chose some lovely soft material from my Mum's material box. Silky material feels extra nice on your face, but cotton is fine too. I got my Mum to cut out two pieces of this material for my eye pillows. The pieces need to be both the same size and long enough to just cover your eyes, and then about the width of your Mum's finger. I enjoyed sewing the two pieces of material together. I had to make sure the material was inside out, so the stitches wouldn't show on the outside. Mum helped make sure my stitches were nice and strong and checked that there weren't any gaps for the lavender to fall through. I left a little gap in one side and then turn the material the right way around and poured in the lavender and flax seeds through the gap. Then I sewed up the gap and my eye pillows were finished! I put some relaxing music on and lay down with my eye pillows on and relaxed.

Sometimes I put the eye bag on the radiator so it warms up and makes the lavender smell extra lovely. I've been told that lavender is really good for taking away stress. It works for me! Sometimes when I have had a stressful day at school, it's all I need to make me feel better. It's good too because it blocks the light out, so even in the summer when the sun is bright in my room, I put my pillow over my eyes and I get some rest from the light!

I FEEL CALM.

 I FEEL CALM.

How to be mindful

We have a new subject at school called 'mindfulness' and it is all about noticing what is around you. It is a really simple way of noticing the things in your life and appreciating them. You'd love it! Sometimes, it is easy to take what we have for granted and walk around moaning or not thinking positively.

Being mindful can also be about living in the moment and enjoying things in the now. All you have to do to get started is practice some breathing techniques. Breathe in the atmosphere around you. What do you notice? What are the colors in the room? How do they make you feel? When we are aware of how we think and feel about something, we are able to be in control of our moods and we can manage the swings and the highs and lows.

Being mindful is really good for helping you be stress-free because it helps you focus on the moment instead of thinking about things that have wound you up. Try it! A really easy way to start is to walk up to an object in your room and just look at it. You might feel silly at first but give it a chance. Breathe in and look at the object. What color is it? What shape is it? What does it feel like? You will notice that you have stopped worrying about other things and afterwards you will feel much calmer. Sometimes, taking a break from your worries can help you realize that they are not worth worrying about in the first place!

Here's another mindfulness exercise. Ask someone to read it out to you:

Sit comfortably in your chair, uncross your legs and place your feet firmly on the ground. Move your body to make it comfortable. Close your eyes and place your hands on your stomach or your lap. Feel yourself becoming calm and relaxed. Take in a deep breath and breathe all the way out. As you sit there, feel your mind becoming still and quiet.

Become aware of how you are sitting and make yourself as comfortable as possible. Notice any tension in your body. Become aware of the floor beneath you. Notice how your feet touch the floor. Move your toes a little as you become more and more grounded and aware of your feet on the floor. Become aware of the chair and how your body is seated on the chair. Become aware of your clothes and how they touch your skin. Spend some time feeling your clothes against your skin. Notice things that you would not have noticed before. Become aware of the temperature in the room. Stay still and just notice the temperature. Is it cool? Is it warm? Is it hot? How warm or cool is your body compared to the room?

Become aware of what is happening inside your body. Stay still and quiet as you notice what is going on inside. Become aware of the internal organs in your body. Spend a few moments being quiet and focused and observing what is going on inside. Notice the details. The more you become mindful, the more calm and relaxed you will feel.

I am mindful. I am mindful.

How to use the

happiness switch

This exercise is really good because it helps you get out of a bad mood and you can do it wherever you are. I love it. If I am stressed out, I just press my happiness switch and then I am back to normal!

All you have to do is think about a time that you were really happy. It could be when you were playing with your friends or a nice day out with your family. I think about a time when me and lots of friends went to the park and we spent the whole afternoon there, playing on the swings and having a picnic. The sun was out, there were no other kids at the park so we had it all to ourselves and my mum had packed my favorite sandwiches, so everything was perfect. She even packed little homemade jellies as a surprise.

As you remember your happy memory, close your eyes and imagine that you are there. Think about what you felt like and how happy you were and really remember how great it was. Try and make everything in the memory really bright and exciting, make all the colors that you can see brighter and the noises even louder than they were. Make all the tastes stronger and the smells stronger too. Then, squeeze your thumb and first finger together while you think about your happy memory. This is your happiness switch.

This was a really happy day that I like to remember

28

Next time that you feel sad, all you have to do is close your eyes. Then put your thumb and first finger together again and you will remember your happy memory.

Like this!

You can be anywhere in the world and you can use your happiness switch and you will feel great. Even if you are having a bad day! It is so easy, don't you think?

 I love the happiness switch because it is calming and relaxing. I can turn my happiness switch on if I feel sad.

Olivia Kutcher age 6 and a half.

I am happy.

I am happy.

Happiness Switch

HOW TO USE
POSITIVE AFFIRMATIONS

Have you noticed that sometimes there is a little voice in your head that says negative things like, 'You can't do it', 'You are not good enough', or 'You are stupid'? I used to have that little voice in my mind all the time. Then I learnt how to use positive affirmations.

We did them in our Relax Kids class. I love positive affirmations. It makes me feel really good about myself. My Relax Kids teacher told us that an affirmation is a positive word or sentence that you repeat to yourself to help you feel better.

Just as we need healthy food to help our bodies grow strong and healthy, we need positive and happy thoughts to help our minds so we can grow up feeling strong and confident inside. Did you know that top athletes and even actors and pop stars use affirmations to help them achieve their goals and improve their performance?

I am kind and helpful.

I am strong.

I am amazing.

I believe in myself.

I have many talents.

Here are our affirmation cards which Mum made us.

My teacher said that when we say something positive there is a change in our body and we release happy chemicals that make us feel great. Isn't that amazing?

The more we think happy and positive thoughts, the more likely we are to say positive words and perform positive actions. Every day when I wake up, I choose an affirmation and repeat it 3 times and I repeat it again with my Mum or Dad before I go to sleep. Here are some of my favorite affirmations:

I AM CONFIDENT AND BELIEVE IN MYSELF

I FEEL CALM AND RELAXED

I RELAX AND LET GO

I AM COOL AND CALM

I AM STRONG AND HEALTHY

I KNOW THAT EVERYTHING IS OK

I AM BRILLIANT

I AM OK. I AM OK.

How to have a positive thought each day

It's important to be able to think positively, because if it is raining and grey then you need to still be happy and not get upset about it or let it ruin your day. This is actually really easy because the world is full of nice words and good things, you just have to take the time to think about them!

There are lots of things that you can do to help you think positively. At school, my teacher writes a positive thought on the board and we all share that thought and think about how it affects us. This is good because it makes the whole class happy at the same time.

Every morning when I wake up I tell myself an affirmation to get me through the day. Yesterday, I chose to say, 'I am strong' because I was helping my Dad in the garden that day. It doesn't really matter if you tell yourself the same thing as the day before, but it is nice to find new things about yourself.

I am a calm star

I am a strong star

At breakfast, my Mum or Dad asks me to pick one of my Relax Kids Star Cards and I take it with me in my coat pocket and at the end of the day, I tell them how it worked for me. Sometimes they say things like 'I am a talented star', 'I am a clever star' or 'I am a creative star.' Yesterday I picked 'I am a co-operative star' and when I got home, I told Mum about how I had helped some of my friends in the school garden. It's really nice and it makes me feel like I am very special because I have been nice to others. It is so easy to be positive. Once you start, you will want to do it more!

I AM POSITIVE.

I AM POSITIVE.

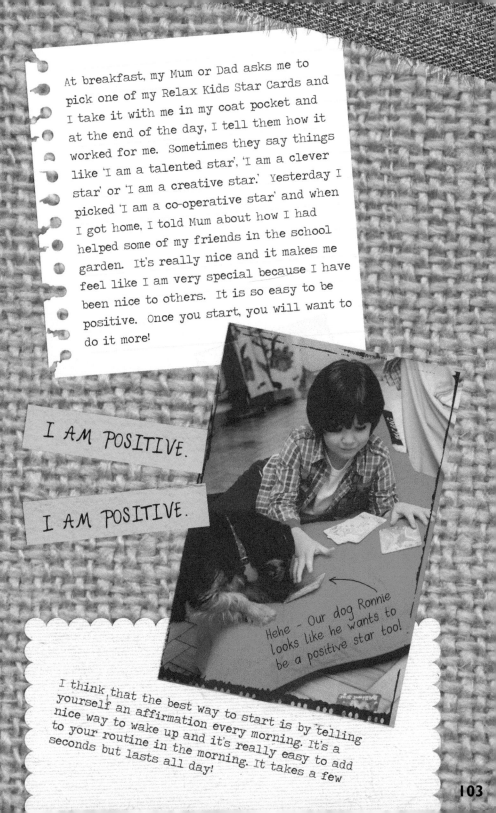

Hehe - Our dog Ronnie looks like he wants to be a positive star too!

I think that the best way to start is by telling yourself an affirmation every morning. It's a nice way to wake up and it's really easy to add to your routine in the morning. It takes a few seconds but lasts all day!

How to make 3 wishes

Sometimes we take things for granted. But we are all very lucky really and remembering that will help stop us getting into a mood over silly things. You always hear people saying that they wish that they had this or that, but you don't always hear people saying that they are thankful for what they have got, which is a bit sad really! My Dad says, 'People always think the grass is greener on the other side, but when they get there it isn't'. It is supposed to mean that you should stop looking for other things and enjoy what you have got.

This is a really nice activity to try. When everyone all over the world does nice things, the world is a much nicer place.

1. Make a wish for yourself. THINK BIG! It can be anything that you can dream of! Mine is to one day swim with a dolphin. I would love to do that and think it would be so much fun. This wish is fun and keeps me smiling because I know I might be able to do it someday!

2. Make a wish for someone you know. Is there someone who needs you to send them some positive thoughts? I wished that my grandma would win her painting competition because she worked really hard on it. I told her my wish and she said that she was so pleased I had wished it for her!

3. Make a wish for the world. What would you like to change in the world? Think positive thoughts about this wish and things will start happening. My wish is that more places like the jungle and parks will be looked after. I think about it all the time, because we only have one world and we need to look after it.

Here is out wishing tree at home.

We made a wishing tree at home out of branches from the garden. We wrote our wishes down and hung them on the wishing tree to remind us of our wishes and to keep thinking positively so that they might come true. My Dad says if we all think positive thoughts, things will start to change and we will be the happiest group of people on the planet!

My friend has a wishing jar for her wishes. She decorated it with glitter and glass paint, so it looks really magical when the light shines through it on the windowsill! She wants to keep her all wishes secret, so instead of writing them down, she drops a button or a charm into the a special jar every time she makes a wish. Only she knows what her wishes are, but the buttons and charms are there so she knows she has made them and she can remember to try and make them come true!

My mind is powerful.

My mind is powerful.

HOW TO MEDITATE

My Mum used to be really stressed, but then she started meditation and now she knows how to stay calm. She does it for ten minutes every day now and says it really helps her at work. We do simple meditation in Relax Kids classes. It feels so good and it actually helps the brain which is amazing! It's easy to start meditating. You just have to find a quiet place and sit very still with your eyes closed and concentrate.

Sometimes it's hard to concentrate. My teacher made a mind jar to show us about concentration. She got a jar full of glitter and water and shook it so that the glitter was dancing about in the jar. After a while, it calmed down and sunk to the bottom of the jar and the water was clear again. She said our minds are like the jar and the glitter is our thoughts. Meditation helps us to calm our thoughts so that our minds are clear and we can concentrate.

Here is my brother using my mind jar.

106

You can meditate by concentrating on your breathing. It's that simple! Breathe in slowly and breathe out slowly and just try to only concentrate on that. I find that I become really calm when I do it.

I also learnt how to meditate with a mantra. A mantra is when you repeat lovely words. I like repeating the word 'peace'. I say, 'peace, peace, peace, peace' in my mind over and over and over and over again. It is amazing - after a while I really do feel peace inside.

Here we are meditating in our Relax Kids class.

Here is one of my favorite meditations. It was written by my friend Amber. She's a really fantastic writer, don't you think? Why don't you get someone to read it to you?

Close your eyes and imagine you are at the bottom of a hill. You are about to climb to the top of it. Now you start to climb. As you climb you feel a slight breeze whipping your hair about. You look up at the forget-me-not blue sky, you see fluffy white clouds shaped like sheep dancing in blue flowers. Then you see a nice area of grass, you lie down on it. You close your eyes and listen to the buzzing of a bee near you collecting some pollen. Listening a bit more, you can hear the calls of lots of different birds calling to each other. Now you get up and climb the rest of the way to the top. Finally you reach the last step. You feel very proud of yourself because you have reached the top of the hill. You look around and can see such a long way. All the fields look like a big patchwork quilt sewn together by hedges, trees and bushes. All the cars and buses are so small they look like ants busy at work. You look at the lovely view and feel the peace and calm up here. Lie down at the top of the hill and repeat, 'I AM SURROUNDED BY PEACE. I AM SURROUNDED BY PEACE' in your mind.

relax Kids CLASSES

Send your child to a magical Relax Kids class!

Movement and games, stretching and massage, breathing, affirmations and visualisations.

Let your child feel GREAT!

I ♥ RK

www.relaxkids.com/class

Breathing exercises

More Relax Kids books and CDs to help children manage anxiety and stress, improve sleep and build self-esteem!

Do you think you have the potential to make a positive difference to children's lives?   BECOME A RELAX KIDS COACH!

Our training course will show you how to teach children important relaxation techniques that will last them a lifetime!

Discover the unique 7-step Relax Kids method for complete relaxation, including movement, games, stretching, massage, breathing exercises, positive affirmations and calming visualisations. Our exercises and resources will also help boost children's confidence, creativity, and self-esteem.

Join over 900 qualified coaches worldwide! Take the first steps towards improving children's futures by finding out more at

www.relaxkids.com/teach

RELAX KIDS PRODUCTS

BOOKS

Aladdin's Magic Carpet
52 fairytale meditations
(ages 3+)

The Wishing Star
52 meditations for children
(ages 5+)

The Pants of Peace
52 meditation exercises for children
(ages 6+)

The Magic Box
52 creative visualisations and
positive affirmations for children
(ages5+)

Be Brilliant
52 pull-out affirmation games, cards
and activities for children
(ages 4+)

CDs

Little Stars (under 5s)
Princesses
Superheroes
Up Up and Away

Nature
Relax and De-stress
Believe and Achieve

Self-Esteem
Concentration
Anger Management
Anxiety and Worry

CARDS

Star Cards - a treasure box of 52 cards to help
children see and develop their inner qualities

Download a FREE relaxation pack
www.relaxkids.com

Testimonials

'This book helps you create that special family time that will capture precious childhood memories to treasure.' Gillian

'A fun, imaginative and practical book that helps create the quality time your children want.' Mrs Fitzroy

'ADDRESS THE FAMILY STRESS WITH THESE LOVELY SIMPLE IDEAS THAT ARE FUN TO DO AND AT THE SAME TIME NURTURE QUALITIES WE WISH TO SEE IN OUR CHILDREN AND OURSELVES.' LORNA HARGREAVE

'My kids love this book! It's simple, practical, a bit different and helps with the 'what are we doing today question?' from your children.' Rachel Mackie

Endorsements

I am always amazed by Marneta's creativity. It's as if she is being 'called' to fulfill a vital mission in our chaotic world: to help our children relax. If there was to be a new comic book character required to join Spiderman and Wonderwoman, a character whose mission was to champion children's battle against the stresses and strains of living in the modern world, Marneta would get the job in an instant!

Mike George
Author of The Immune System of the Soul

Marneta is one of the most happy and beautiful people I know and this is reflected in all of her books. The book is just gorgeous to look at and is crammed full of information that I know will make so many children feel happier and in turn make their parent's lives a little easier, bringing families closer together. Who wouldn't want that? Marneta has done a great job as always!

Sarah Newton Teen and Parenting Expert

When Marneta Viegas tells me that she has written another book I get very excited as I know it will be full of wonderfully creative ideas, magical moments and sparkly positivity. Once again Marneta has created a really helpful resource for children, and for parents, that will inspire, motivate and nurture everyone's self esteem and will help to develop a positive mindset so necessary in today's hectic, frantic, busy world.

Sue Atkins
ITV "This Morning" Parenting Expert

I love this book! simple. practical. a bit different and helps with the 'what are we doing today question?' from your children. It is fun. imaginative and practical and perfect for creating quality time with your children.

Jill. Parent

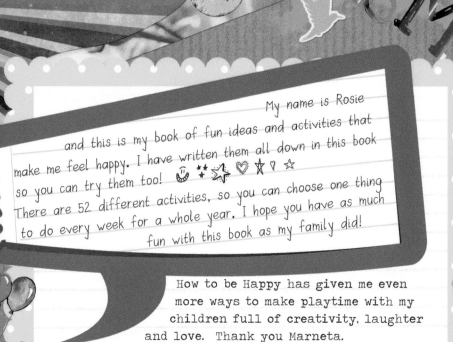

My name is Rosie and this is my book of fun ideas and activities that make me feel happy. I have written them all down in this book so you can try them too! There are 52 different activities, so you can choose one thing to do every week for a whole year. I hope you have as much fun with this book as my family did!

How to be Happy has given me even more ways to make playtime with my children full of creativity, laughter and love. Thank you Marneta.
ROBERT HOLDEN, author of Happiness NOW and Loveability

I believe that happiness should be taught to children of all ages. Relax Kids does just that!
DR DAVID R HAMILTON, author of Why Kindness is Good for You and How your Mind can Heal your Body

The book is just gorgeous to look at and is crammed full of ideas that will make so many children feel happier and bring families closer together. Who wouldn't want that?
SARAH NEWTON, Celebrity Parenting Expert

Once again Marneta has created a really helpful resource for children, and for parents, that will inspire, motivate and nurture everyone's self-esteem and will help to develop a positive mindset so necessary in today's hectic, frantic, busy world.
SUE ATKINS, ITV "This Morning" Parenting Expert

OUR STREET
BOOKS

Our Street Books for children of all ages, deliver a potent mix of
fantastic, rip-roaring adventure and fantasy stories to excite the
imagination; spiritual fiction to help the mind and the heart
grow; humorous stories to make the funny bone grow; historical
tales to evolve interest; and all manner of subjects that stretch
imagination, grab attention, inform, inspire and keep the pages
turning. Our subjects include Non-fiction and Fiction, Fantasy
and Science Fiction, Religious, Spiritual, Historical, Adventure,
Social Issues, Humour, Folk Tales and more.

RELAX KIDS TITLES

Relax Kids: Aladdin's Magic Carpet

Let Snow White, the Wizard of Oz and other fairytale characters
show you and your child how to meditate and relax.
Marneta Viegas

Using well-known and loved fairy stories this is a gentle and
fun way of introducing children to the world of meditation and
relaxation. It is designed to counteract some of the tensions with
which we are all familiar at the end of a busy day, and offer
parent and children, from 3 upwards, together some quality
time to relax and share. The meditations and visualisations aim
to develop children's imagination and provide them with skills
that will be invaluable for the rest of their life. Using 52 fairy
stories and nursery rhymes like flying on Aladdin's magic
carpet, climbing Jack's beanstalk, flying through the air like
Peter Pan, swimming in the ocean with the Little Mermaid,
asking a question of the Wizard of Oz, listening to the sounds of
the forest with Snow White, and many others, children are
encouraged to go on magical journeys in the mind.
Hardcover: December 4, 2003 978-1-90381-666-0 $14.95 £9.99.
Paperback: November 28, 2014, ISBN: 978-1-78279-869-9,
$14.95 £9.99

Relax Kids: The Magic Box

Dip into a box of visualisation delights with these unique Relax
Kids meditations
Marneta Viegas

52 meditations for children (ages 5+)
The Magic Box is full of creative visualisations, meditations and
relaxations. Children can imagine they are on a tropical island,
flying into space, in a hot air balloon, time travelling and

leaving their worries on the worry tree. The book combines fantasy story meditations with deep relaxations, simple mindfulness exercises and positive affirmations. It is a great way to introduce meditation and mindfulness to young children.

Practiced regularly, these exercises can have a profound effect on children's mental, emotional and physical wellbeing.

Paperback: March 28, 2014 978-1-78279-187-4 $14.95 £9.99.

Relax Kids: The Wishing Star

Helping wishes and dreams come true with positive thinking, guided visualisations and affirmations for children

Marneta Viegas

Using guided meditations based around traditional stories this is a gentle and fun way of introducing older children to the world of meditation and relaxation. It is designed to counteract some of the tensions with which we are all familiar at the end of a busy day, and offer parent and children together some quality time to relax and share. The meditations and visualisations aim to develop children's imagination and provide them with skills that will be invaluable for the rest of their life.

For children aged 5 upwards.

Hardcover: January 20, 2005 978-1-90381-677-6 $14.95 £9.99. **Paperback:** November 28, 2014, ISBN: 978-1-78279-870-5, $14.95 £9.99.

Relax Kids: The Little Book of Stars

Helping children see their true star quality with simple visualisation exercises.

Marneta Viegas

The Little Book of Stars is the perfect way to introduce toddlers to relaxation and meditation. Each page explores a positive quality or value in an easy-to-understand and child friendly way. Examples include Happy Star, Calm Star, Brilliant Star and Generous Star. This book is designed to engage very young children while introducing them to simple relaxation and mindfulness techniques. Each relaxation exercise takes around 3-5 mins. The exercises in the book also aim help develop children's sense of awareness and self worth so promoting confidence and self-esteem. This book can be used at home, before nap time or bedtime or in nursery and kindergarten schools. Ages 2-5

Paperback: November 28, 2014, ISBN: 978-1-78279-460-8, **Price:** $ 14.95 £ 9.99

Relax Kids: How to be Happy

Teaching children the true meaning of happiness and helping them create happy family moments at home.

52 positive activities for children

Marneta Viegas

How to be Happy is a scrap book bursting with positive ideas, simple and economical activities and fun games. Each page includes colourful pictures and diagrams to explain the activity in simple child-like language. There are some in-book activities but this is mainly a book of ideas. This book is full of interesting ways to relax, have fun and be happy. It encourages spirituality for young children. Each chapter is a different activity such as how to make peace pebbles, how to make a chill out corner, how to be kind, how to relax, how to manage stress, how to write a personal prayer, how to make worry dolls. The book is written in child language and so would be easily accessible to young families. It makes it easy for families to embrace simple spirituality, acts of kindness and spiritual activities. The book is designed to bring families together and allow children to enjoy spending quality time with their parents. It aims to help children manage their worries, anxiety and emotions whilst helping them grow up to be confident and happy.

Ages 4-7

Paperback: December 12, 2014, ISBN: 978-1-78279-162-1,
$ 19.95 £ 9.99

Relax Kids: Pants of Peace

Allowing children to enter the world of their imagination with positive thinking and visualisations

52 meditation tools for children

Marneta Viegas

An innovative book that helps children get in touch with a wide range of inner qualities and values through creative meditation and affirmations exercises. Examples include shoe of confidence, cloak of protection, pen of appreciation and hat of happiness. Each meditation takes a positive quality or value and shows children in a creative and imaginative way how to develop that quality to improve their own life. This book encourages children to enjoy moments of calm and also helps develop their imaginations in a world of electronic gadgets. Pants of Peace is perfect for parents and teachers to read with children. The exercises are a toolkit to help develop children's mental health and well-being. Regular listening to these simple meditations can help children become more self-aware, positive and confident. This book can be used at home to help children relax or in the classroom. Ages 6+ The Relax Kids series is currently available in Europe and will be available in US from 2015.

Paperback: August 29, 2014, ISBN: 978-1-78279-199-7,
$ 14.95 £ 9.99

CD available at http://www.relaxkids.com/UK/Audio CDs